Capitalism – a Condensed Version

Capitalism – a Condensed Version

ARTHUR SELDON

WITH COMMENTARIES BY JAMES BARTHOLOMEW
AND D. R. MYDDELTON

The Institute of Economic Affairs

First published in Great Britain in 2007 by
The Institute of Economic Affairs
2 Lord North Street
Westminster
London SW1P 3LB
in association with Profile Books Ltd

The mission of the Institute of Economic Affairs is to improve public
understanding of the fundamental institutions of a free society, by analysing
and expounding the role of markets in solving economic and social problems.

A CIP catalogue record for this book is available from the British Library.

ISBN-10: 0 255 36598 5
ISBN-13: 978 0 255 36598 7

Many IEA publications are translated into languages other than English or
are reprinted. Permission to translate or to reprint should be sought from the
Director General at the address above.

Typeset in Stone by MacGuru Ltd
info@macguru.org.uk

Printed and bound in Great Britain by Hobbs the Printers

CONTENTS

THE AUTHOR

Arthur Seldon (1916–2005) was Founder President of the IEA and was its Editorial Director from 1959 to 1988. He was also a staff examiner at the London School of Economics (1956–66), a member of the BMA Committee on Health Financing (1968–70) and vice-president of the Mont Pèlerin Society (1980–86). He received honorary degrees from University Francisco Marroquin, Guatemala, and Buckingham University, and an honorary fellowship from the London School of Economics. Arthur Seldon published widely on a range of subjects related to the role of markets in solving economic and social problems. He was appointed CBE in 1983.

FOREWORD

This monograph is a masterly condensation of Arthur Seldon's original text on 'capitalism'. It is lucid, well organised and contains a great deal of interesting material. It is a strong statement of the evils of collectivism. David Moller should be congratulated for producing this fine work from Arthur Seldon's original book.

This monograph will be effective in communicating Arthur Seldon's message to the ordinary layman, at the same time that its analytical rigour allows it to be used at all levels of intellectual debate. It is an authoritative, informed and passionate statement of the case for capitalism and the case against collectivism. This condensed version of *Capitalism* is clear, well written and straightforward. It deserves a large audience.

PROFESSOR MILTON FRIEDMAN
Senior Research Fellow
Hoover Institution
Stanford University
California
USA
July 2006

The views expressed in this monograph are, as in all IEA publications, those of the authors and not those of the Institute (which has no corporate view), its managing trustees, Academic Advisory Council Members or senior staff.

9

SUMMARY

- Capitalism is the only economic system that preserves individual freedom while raising living standards.
- The industrial revolution, and the consequent rise in prosperity, would never have taken place under either the medieval guilds or state socialism.
- Inequality is a necessary result of allowing people to advance as individuals in the market. Measures to enforce equality slow down progress and innovation, harming everyone.
- Individual property rights provide incentives for owners to conserve and improve their assets. Collective or 'public' ownership leads to neglect and the waste of resources.
- Market prices enable the collection and exploitation of scattered knowledge about people's preferences. Socialist central planners have no comparable device for obtaining this information.
- Rationing by price has many advantages over political rationing. So-called 'free' services, such as the National Health Service, induce waste and mutual impoverishment.
- Capitalism puts man's long-term interest as consumer above his interest as producer. In contrast, state socialism puts jobs before services and governments tend to favour organised producer interests over consumers.
- For capitalism to yield its best results, the political process

must be confined to organising the minimal duties of the state, such as defence, where the market may not be able to operate. The living standards of the West are still restrained and unnecessarily unequal because the political process has too many beneficiaries.

- The welfare state has largely destroyed the voluntary provision of services, such as education and health, which preceded it. In the absence of the market, quality of service has suffered, producer interests have triumphed and the Victorian culture of 'self-reliance' has been undermined.
- A world of capitalist countries is more likely to be peaceful than a world of socialist states. Individuals and private firms, including multinationals, trading in an international market, have a clear vested interest in favour of world peace.

Capitalism – a Condensed Version

1 INTRODUCTION

John Blundell[1] and Philip Booth[2]

The origin of *Capitalism – a Condensed Version*

At an IEA event to celebrate Liberty Fund's publication of the *Collected Works* of Arthur Seldon,[3] Ralph Harris, the founding General Director of the IEA, suggested that a condensed version of Arthur Seldon's classic work *Capitalism* should be published. After giving the idea some thought, David Moller, a staff writer for *Reader's Digest* magazine for more than 30 years, was asked to undertake the task. He has produced a brilliant summary of the original book, in just 10,000 words, which captures its essence perfectly. The text is a fine antidote to the anti-capitalist rhetoric that is so common in the media – particularly in so-called public service broadcasting, in state schools and among the political establishment.

We hope that this new publication will particularly inspire young people. *Capitalism – a Condensed Version* should give young people who are already favourably inclined towards the market economy the ammunition to defend it and to attack the

1 John Blundell is Director General of the Institute of Economic Affairs.

2 Philip Booth is Editorial and Programme Director of the Institute of Economic Affairs and Professor of Insurance and Risk Management at the Sir John Cass Business School, City University.

3 The *Collected Works* are contained in seven volumes and are available through the IEA's website: www.iea.org.uk.

alternatives. And it should also help young people to understand the shortcomings of the alternative models of organising society. It is ironic that, at the age when young people often go through a rebellious phase, they also seem most inclined to embrace models of economic, political and social organisation that allow them the least possible freedom to pursue their own goals. This monograph explains how, whatever the shortcomings of capitalism, the alternatives are worse.

The structure of *Capitalism – a Condensed Version*

After a brief introduction to the history of capitalism there is a discussion of the essential features of a market economy: property, the price mechanism, change and inequality. Many do not like what they regard as the spectre of inequality that hangs over capitalist societies. Yet the alternatives – whereby politicians and bureaucrats are responsible for the allocation of economic resources – lead to a levelling down and scarcely less inequality than one sees in capitalist societies.

Another important theme is that capitalism delivers what consumers want. Whether it is good books, dishwashers or iPods, producers in a capitalist society have to act in the service of consumers. It is not politicians, or firms, who decide what is to be produced – it is the people. This contrasts, for example, with what we see in today's welfare state, where health services are offered on a 'take it or leave it' basis. And it contrasts markedly with what we see in the UK's state education system, which is much less market-oriented than almost any other in western Europe and is foisted upon parents and students, with the very people whom the system is designed to benefit having the least control of what is offered.

Indeed, as Seldon demonstrates, it is one of the great lies of the modern age, promoted by those with the strongest vested interests, that there was no welfare before the welfare state. The reality is different. The record of private sector provision in pensions, housing, health and education, in an age when national income was much lower, was truly remarkable. Given the conditions of the time the achievements of private sector welfare were far greater than those of the fossilised state institutions we see today.

Seldon ends by making clear that capitalism is not perfect. The phrase 'the pursuit of the perfect is the enemy of the good' could have been designed to describe the actions of those who continually try to use the power of the state to make the outcomes of a market economy closer to some theoretically perfect vision. The market has self-correcting mechanisms, particularly through the development of deeper and more sophisticated property rights and the use of the price mechanism, to bring forth more supply and ration demand in times of relative scarcity. Government action has no such self-correcting mechanisms and efforts by government to 'correct' the outcomes of markets frequently have precisely the reverse of the intended effects.

David Moller has done a remarkable job in editing Arthur Seldon's original work to just 10,000 words. The editor has included page numbers from the original work to allow readers to refer back to find further insights, further references and to understand the original context. The version to which the page numbers refer is that published in *The Collected Works of Arthur Seldon, Volume 1 – The Virtues of Capitalism.* The original version of *Capitalism* appears in Part 2 of that volume, pp. 53–436.

Commentaries

We asked two commentators to write essays examining the issues raised by Arthur Seldon's *Capitalism*. The first, by James Bartholomew (Chapter 3), asks why capitalism is so derided in society, despite its manifest successes in bringing prosperity to those who could never have had any hope of improvements in their standard of living without the market economy. He also examines the problems of government provision of welfare and the strengths of private provision. As he notes, the fact that the private sector provided welfare services efficiently to people at all levels of income has more or less been written out of history.

D. R. Myddelton (Chapter 4) examines how capitalism can be, or perhaps is being, brought down. Politicians do not stand for election with big programmes to circumscribe our freedoms. Instead, they turn the tide by stealth: by small incremental measures that erode liberty, sometimes in a sufficiently fundamental way (such as by passing retrospective legislation) that a nail is firmly hammered into the coffin of capitalism.

But capitalism is resourceful because people are resourceful. So, even in the most difficult of circumstances, it can be possible to turn back the tide of socialism so that people can once again be freed to better their condition. D. R. Myddelton is not wrong, but we should be optimistic, just as Arthur Seldon was optimistic. We should continue the struggle just as those who overthrew the harsher versions of socialism – communism and Nazism – continued the struggle in the twentieth century. Against the odds they prevailed, so that the resourcefulness of free peoples could be liberated in the face of oppressive government.

D. R. Myddelton has also kindly provided the Questions for Discussion.

Capitalism is an excellent introduction to the power of the market economy to better the human condition. It should bolster the arguments of seasoned writers in this field. It provides a summary of the arguments for the interested non-economist. Perhaps most importantly, it should assist young people in understanding why an economy that is not consciously directed by 'organisers', where people are left free to pursue their own objectives subject to their not interfering with the property or freedom of others, raises the welfare of all.

2   CAPITALISM[1]

Capitalist beginnings

Capitalism requires not defence but celebration. Its achievement in creating high and rising living standards for the masses without sacrificing personal liberty speaks for itself (p. 55).[2] It is the instrument which people in all societies and stages of economic development instinctively use to escape from want and enrich one another by exchange (p. 61).

For two centuries, it has displayed steady, though fluctuating, development despite wars, political convulsions, bloody revolutions, and most damaging, the unremitting but misleading condemnation by the world's outstanding philosophers and scientists. Indeed, capitalism has had an intellectual triumph over its alternative – the socialism now being rejected by people on every continent (p. 56).

Capitalism forged ahead in the eighteenth century under the impetus of the technological revolution. The early inventions of

---

1   *Capitalism* was condensed by David Moller, who is a former staff writer for *Reader's Digest*.

2   Page numbers have been inserted to aid the reader who wishes to refer to the original text. The version to which the page numbers refer is that published in *The Collected Works of Arthur Seldon, Volume 1: The Virtues of Capitalism*. The original version of *Capitalism* by Arthur Seldon appears in Part 2 of that volume, pp. 53–436.

the 1760s and later created enterprises that were financed, partly or largely, by private loans from family, friends and neighbours. Then in the 1850s came the company laws that created joint-stock firms, with limited liability, to encourage strangers to lend and invest (p. 215).

The consequent widening Industrial Revolution drew people in from the primitive dwellings of the countryside to the more substantial homes of the towns. It replaced coarse apparel by woven clothes. It replaced the endless hours of cottage working by legislation on factory hours. It also provided drainage and public order for the large numbers now crowded into towns (p. 207).

The new conditions of urban living were still often grim – but to blame them on capitalism is as plausible as blaming every human advance for its incidental disadvantages, unforeseen but temporary until new measures can be organised to remove them (p. 207).

Marxist misinformation

Many, however, have continued to condemn capitalism, and urge socialism, without putting two key questions asked and answered by liberal economists (p. 208) (The word 'liberal' is used here in its classical European sense, and not in the British party-political illiberal distortion or in the American sense where it is virtually a euphemism for 'socialist') (p. 82).

First, would the eventual rise in living standards have taken place without capitalism? The answer is that it would not have done under the medieval guilds or under state socialism. Second, would the tasks of organising urban living have been foreseen or accomplished better under socialism? The answer is that its record, wherever it has been introduced in the world, indicates no reasons to suppose that it would have been more prescient, prompt or proficient (p. 208).

The Marxists have made much of the fall in general incomes in some periods. But it was hardly likely that the new conditions of industry and work would proceed uninterruptedly — and the notion that socialism proceeds smoothly upwards without fluctuations is a myth (p. 209). Indeed, it not only suffers from unemployment and inflation but often compounds the offence by disguising their evidence and suppressing statistics (p. 69).

Yet Marxists have been disposed to see almost every capitalist downturn as terminal — from the first crisis observed by the socialist Friedrich Engels in 1844, to the Great Depression of 1929–31 and stock-market crash of October 1987 (pp. 209, 426).

The spur of inequality

Marxists have also often criticised capitalism for its lack of equality. Yet the history of Europe demonstrates that inequality is necessary to reveal progress by different people and reward those who take the risks of trying new ways of solving known tasks (p. 213).

It is also essential to stimulate emulation, from which all eventually gain. When, say, one farmer forged ahead, the information costs of learning about the effects of new methods were lowered for all the others. Productivity and living standards improved all round. If equality is enforced by socialist law, or encouraged by conservative custom, it slows down or suppresses progress. The peoples of Europe would have remained poorer longer (p. 213).

Allowing people to advance as individuals in the market,

without waiting for others, is in the end more egalitarian than the socialist method of waiting for agreement, universal or by majorities, in debating chambers. For as others follow, more can share in the advance. Inequality in action is the way to equality in result (p. 213).

These facts notwithstanding, the reputation of capitalism has suffered from the continuing influence of Marxist history. It is still taught widely in the Western world. It is still fallacious. And it still cannot explain why the world aspires to capitalism, especially where it has experienced socialism (p. 209).

The importance of property

A crucial difference between capitalism and socialism is in the role of property (p. 209). Indeed, it was the refinement of property rights in the nineteenth century which was probably more important even than technological advances in helping capitalism realise its full potential (p. 215).

For while the real owners in capitalism take care of their property or other assets, the nominal owners in socialism cannot because they do not know what they own. What belongs nominally to everyone on paper belongs in effect to no one in practice. Coalfields, railways, schools and hospitals that are owned 'by the people' are in real life owned by phantoms. No nominal owner can sell, hire, lend, bequeath or give them to family, friends or good causes. Public ownership is a myth and a mirage (p. 210).

The effort required to 'care' for, say, the 60-millionth individual share of a hospital or school owned by 60 million Britons (updated figure), even if identifiable, would far outweigh the benefit; so it is not made, even if it could be. The task is deputed to public servants answerable to politicians who in turn are in socialist mythology answerable to the people (p. 210).

In this long line of communication the citizen is often in effect disenfranchised. The wonder is that the myth of 'public ownership' continues to be propagated by men and women who aspire to political leadership. In commercial advertising, it would be denounced as a fraud on the people (p. 210).

When the break-up of the former Soviet Union induced Russians to release even unfavourable information, few were surprised to learn that the productivity of privately owned plots in the USSR had been ten to twenty times that of 'publicly owned' land (p. 211).

Yet socialists have persistently avoided acceptance of the truth that public property destroys the essence of property. Changing private identifiable property into public unidentifiable property is to destroy the incentives to protect, conserve, improve and render it productive by using it profitably in making goods and services for which consumers will pay (p. 187).

The enlightenment of pricing

The essential instrument by which people can do that – and which has enabled capitalism to reach standards of living that are multiples of socialism – is the pricing system of the market. This cannot be used in the centralised form of state socialism because it decentralises the power to make decisions to individual buyers and sellers far from the control of central planners. Neither can it be used in the decentralised form of 'market socialism' that socialist economists have been trying to devise for more than half a century (p. 184).

For a price mechanism requires private property to create and calibrate the incentives to innovate, invest, anticipate demand, adjust supply and take the risks in all these decisions, with rewards for success but penalties for failure. The dilemma is that socialism is founded on public property, which does not reproduce the required incentives, rewards and penalties (p. 186).

Prices have two main functions. The obvious one is to provide income as a result of bargains on wages, salaries, fees, charges, rents and so on. In this form, prices are used in socialism as well as capitalism, but in capitalism they are characteristically decided by agreements between buyers and sellers and in socialism by political decisions (p. 196).

The other function is less obvious but more vital: pricing is the device for collecting and exploiting scattered information. It conveys the vital information on earnings, costs and profits required to reach decisions on what to make, how much to make, at what prices to sell, how much to reinvest and where resources are to be used (pp. 196, 213).

Generally, the higher the price of the product, the more resources are allocated to a use in a firm, an occupation or industry. Socialism has no comparable device: resources are allocated by planners who, since socialist market pricing is impracticable, have no other instrument for discovering individual preferences, which are thus generally ignored (p. 197).

Whatever use central planners make of prices, they are not so much to discover the people's preferences as to conceal the politicians' mistakes. Even where they are used to discourage demand for particularly scarce goods or to encourage demand for goods produced in excessive quantities, the decisions are political, usually to disguise inefficiency in central planning (p. 197).

The information conveyed by prices, or changes in prices, may be unwelcome or disagreeable. The rationing, or changes in availability of goods and services, that they induce may be adverse or harmful to their producers. The signals they represent may induce movement from producing some goods and services to very different goods and services, from comfortable jobs to uncertain new jobs, from familiar to unfamiliar housing and surroundings (p. 197).

This is the source of much antipathy to free markets. It accounts for the resentment against competition, which reveals the firms or industries that fail to adapt themselves most expeditiously to price changes. And it explains the political opposition to the capitalist system which creates the environment for free markets, flexible pricing and economic liberalism generally (p. 197).

The inevitability of change

Political parties of the left hope to exploit the unavoidable discomforts of social and technical change by blaming their Conservative political opponents. Their opponents have not learned to reply that change must take place under all economic systems: the choice is not between change and no change but between the gradual change of a market economy and the arbitrary, unpredictable change of a politicised system in which it is timed to suit political calculation (p. 197).

If the pricing of capitalism is not used, the alternative is the political machinery of socialism, which orders people to produce more, produce less, change their jobs, move homes and generally runs their lives (p. 197).

Rationing by price has so many advantages over political rationing. First, price is neutral: it emerges spontaneously where people who want to sell meet others who want to buy. Price expresses the terms on which they voluntarily exchange. Unless both sides do better, they do not exchange (p. 200).

If there are several buyers or sellers, each seller is protected by all other buyers from accepting too low a price, and each buyer by all other sellers from paying too high a price. Together the buyers and sellers form a market (p. 200).

Price is also cautionary. The buyer will think twice before buying. If there is no price, because he is paying indirectly through government by taxes, he will not think twice, but ask for more services than he 'needs'. The liberal economist Lord Ralph Harris has expressed the principle graphically: 'If it's free, put me down for two' (p. 200).

The humour is moderated, however, when it is recalled that nil pricing, or rather indirect pricing disguised as taxes, can induce waste, callous disregard for the needs of friends and neighbours and in the end a war of all against all in which we impoverish one another. The obvious example is the 'free' National Health Service (NHS), in which we are all tempted to take up the time of over-worked doctors, ask for more pills than we need, stay in hospital longer and use equipment carelessly (p. 200).

'Free' services, in effect, induce irresponsible mutual impoverishment. By destroying information, they generate a society which discounts caring, concern and compassion. Only the market tells the truth that there is not, and cannot be, enough of every medical aid to avoid all pain or save all life. No politician will say that. But by revealing the truth, pricing induces caring for scarce supplies. Politics incites profligacy (p. 200).

Much the same is true of prices artificially depressed, even if the reason seems well intentioned. If the price of renting council house-room is subsidised by rent restriction, so that low-income families can pay depressed rents, they will occupy more space than they require or remain in it longer after their children have grown up and moved. They thus prevent new families with young children from moving into homes with more space (pp. 200, 201).

The better way is to supplement their low income to enable them to pay the market rent. The supplements can also be varied with income. And they can be reduced in time when income rises more easily than artificially low rents can be varied because they create vested interests and are politically difficult to raise, as the British experience demonstrates (p. 201).

The customer just has to be right

In fact, the glory of capitalism is that, more than any other system known to history, it uses the only mechanism that can put man's long-term interest as consumer above his interest as producer (p. 265). Karl Marx was imprisoned by the notion of class interests: in particular, the conflict between the capitalist class and working class (p. 409).

In the real world, the interests of both capitalists and workers differ in each group. The interests of capitalists as sellers make them prefer monopoly; as buyers they prefer competition. Likewise, workers, as sellers of labour, overtly prefer to be organised in monopoly-selling organisations like trade unions; as buyers of the products or services of other workers, they instinctively prefer competition between firms, wholesalers and retailers (p. 409).

Only capitalism can make the consumer in us sovereign, and has in varying degree done so in history, because the competition of the market can prevent us from myopically asserting our interests as producers by protecting established but outdated industries, occupations and jobs. 'Job creation' and 'job protection' are retrogressive impoverishing policies that can be sustained only by the political process. They embody socialist thinking and require state coercion (p. 181).

All other politico-economic systems have subjected man's consumer interest to his producer interest. Feudalism saw the rule of the landowning lord of the manor. Mercantilism was run by producer guilds. Syndicalism envisaged rule by worker-producers. Corporatism sought to combine employers and employees as producers. Municipal socialism ran public utilities as work creators. State socialism ran national industries as job protectors. The British post-war consensus was democratic corporatism. The welfare state has put jobs before services (p. 181).

All these alternatives to the market were and remain myopic expressions of the anxiety to secure the producer interests of owners, employers, traders, merchants or employees. They were and remain protectionist conspiracies or 'rackets' that obstructed change to safeguard established producer expectations. Where they prevailed in the Middle Ages, and in some countries in modern times, they brought stagnation and eventual decay. In time the economy slowed down and seized up (p. 181).

The market is the only mechanism that has evolved to induce man to look to his long-term interests. He does not consume in order to produce. He produces in order to consume (p. 181). The market is uncomfortable. But it produces the high living standards – in food, clothing, shelter, comforts, travel – that producers ultimately want more than their immediate jobs (p. 181).

Politicians too often get it wrong

Sadly, politicians have not always allowed the market to produce its best results. In Britain, the Liberal Party did so for a few decades in the nineteenth century. The Labour Party in its early years in office had some remaining liberals, but was generally the protectionist arm of retrogressive trade unions. The Conservatives in general have had an indifferent record. In the 1930s they sponsored producer protection when they abandoned free trade in 1932, introduced transport licensing, agricultural marketing boards and other 'anti-capitalist' restrictionist policies (p. 181).

Capitalism has not been safe with British politicians until the new Conservatives, non-conformist libertarian Whigs, joined the remaining, paternalistic High Tories in Mrs Thatcher's governments. They made a valiant effort to rid the British economy of a century of over-government, protectionism and over-regulation, and to restore the free markets in which the primary consumer interest in every man can prevail over his myopic producer interest. In ten years it turned the tide in the affairs of men, but it will take many more to liberate and liberalise the British economy (p. 182).

The task is not easy because we all see our producer interest more vividly than our consumer interest. Work is the source of income and of standing in society. The rewards we can reap by prevailing on government to yield to our demands for 'help' are larger than the immediate losses we suffer as consumers (p. 182).

When farmers, doctors, nurses, teachers, university professors or government officials secure larger subsidies, higher pay, shorter hours, longer holidays or better conditions than they are worth, because it is politically expedient to keep them quiet, they gain as producers but lose as consumers in higher taxes or higher prices. Their gain is immediate, apparent and sizeable; their loss is distant, obscure and minuscule (p. 182).

The results are damaging to democracy. Since the cost of pressurising government yields a much larger return in producer gains than it imposes in consumer losses, we tend to organise as producers rather than as consumers. But in the end we all lose far more as consumers than we gain as producers: old industries, firms and occupations are kept alive, government is aggrandised, taxes are inflated, the articulate are incited to organise, the citizen is impelled to take to the streets to gain a hearing, parliament is bypassed (p. 182).

Government: small is beautiful

If capitalism is to yield its best results, so far unrealised anywhere, the political process must be confined to the minimal duties of the state (p. 58). For although government may be indispensable for some purposes – defending the realm, keeping the peace, some pure research, environmental protection – the reason is not that it is superior to the market but that the market cannot work at all (pp. 166, 299).

In short, wherever it is used, government is so disappointing or worse – inefficient, unaccountable and corrupt – that it is best not to use it at all except for functions where all its faults have to be tolerated to obtain the services required (pp. 299, 300).

The political process is worlds apart from the market process. It is the arena of *specialists* – in the arts of persuasion, organisation, infiltration, debate, lobbying, manipulating meetings, moving resolutions at conferences or hard bargaining behind closed doors. The market is the world of *generalists* – ordinary men and women who do their work by day and go home at night (p. 169).

The original inspiration of socialism is the notion that men or women with political power, acquired through the open hustings of electioneering, would use it for the common good. It was always implicit that there would somehow be some magical change in human nature (p. 166).

In fact, this vision of socialism is never likely to become reality until it resolves the unending circular reasoning in which it is entrapped: that human nature will not become selfless until scarcity is replaced by superabundance, but superabundance will not replace scarcity until human nature becomes selfless (p. 282).

The capitalist market depends on no such wishful thinking (p. 166). But far from achieving American President Abraham Lincoln's ideal of a government of the people, by the people, for the people, representative democracy has too often led to a government of the busy, by the bossy, for the bully (p. 172).

Even the most technically immaculate rule risks being misused by politicians. This is not because they are inherently mendacious but because the political process provides so many opportunities in which the misuse of rules is politically profitable in garnering votes, winning time after a bad mistake or stroke of ill luck, or fomenting a short-lived boom before a general election (pp. 300, 301).

One of the politician's most beguiling tricks is the budget deficit. The economic benefits of government expenditure thus go to contemporary citizens, and therefore to the politicians of the time, but the cost is borne by voters of the future. Politicians who are profligate, and live on loans today, may not even be in public life long enough to receive the wrath of the voters of tomorrow.

Little wonder governments often bequeath large debts to their successors (p. 221).

While there is much debate on the need, nature and extent of public spending, the larger part of the public sector in Britain is in fact a political artefact: not an economic necessity or a public preference. There is a long list of services that are not public goods – from most schools and hospitals to housing and pensions, and from public libraries to job centres (p. 230).

Many, like state education, have been defended as the way to deal with poverty, but even when poverty gradually receded from the British scene they were continued – and enlarged – by the momentum of party politics and by unions and other vested interests that found they could extract more from political negotiation with ministers or civil servants than from consumers in the market (p. 230).

In fact, the public sector could now shed many of its duties. Even some functions of the law could be supplied in the market. Congestion in the courts could lead individuals involved in disputes to ask former judges of the high or lower courts, retired or wanting a change, to arbitrate between them (p. 298).

The police could lose much of their protection of persons and property to private agencies. More prisons could be run by private firms. Taxes may have to be levied by government but could be collected by private companies. Fire services are not necessarily public: in Denmark and some towns in the United States they are sometimes supplied by private firms (p. 233).

Universities and other suppliers of higher learning could derive more income from their customers – students, industry or overseas institutions. More cost-covering charging for libraries, museums, art galleries, opera, ballet, beach facilities and many local government services could remove them from the misnomer of public goods and move them to local firms (p. 234).

Indeed, because the public sector has tried to do so much, the efficient supply of public goods 'proper' has often been damaged by the inefficient supply of public goods 'improper' long after they were made superfluous by technical and social advance. It is not therefore surprising that government is slow to ensure the supply of possibly new public goods, such as protection against air or water pollution, coastal preservation and the conservation of ancient buildings or animal species. If it had pruned back the public goods 'improper' over the decades, it might have better anticipated its new tasks (p. 234).

Yet the days of many public goods 'improper' could be numbered. The two largest bastions of the public sector, education and medicine, could be eroded by rising incomes or tax evasion if government continues to prevent escape by enforcing taxes for sink schools or inhospitable hospitals (p. 234).

Costly compassion

Why has the public sector welfare state grown so vast? The resort to government is the characteristic instinct of the socialist mind that until recently had infected politicians of all parties in the West. Certainly, it undermined the development of the voluntary institutions which had been spreading in Britain during an exceptional phase of economic liberalism from the 1830s to the 1880s (p. 178).

The instinct had six main sources: first, the notion that if the market failed, the only alternative was the state; second, the superstition that collective action would secure better use of resources than individual action; third, the myth that public control was more responsible than private; fourth, the non sequitur that, since government was obviously necessary in external defence and internal safety, it could also properly supply many other services; fifth, the wishful thinking that, since government has the resources to create good works, able people should join to ensure that it did; sixth, the self-delusion that government is the arena of professionally inclined people who would rather provide a service to others than work for profit for themselves (p. 178).

The services of mercy, compassion, equity and universal benevolence have been given a warm-sounding name, 'welfare', that begs the question not asked by the socialist mind: whether they are what the people would have wanted for themselves if they had been allowed to decide. They are called by a name that reflects the salesmanship of politics: the welfare state suggests that the services supplied outside the state are less desirable, commendable or beneficial (p. 306).

Because the welfare state is organised by public servants they are supposed to do public good. Yet the beneficiaries for whom they are supplied would not be anxious to keep them, or to oppose reform, if they knew their opportunity cost – what else they could have had for their taxes (p. 306).

A makeover for the welfare state

The suggested privatisation of the welfare state, and its substantial transfer to the market, is a proposition that will shock most politicians, all officials and bureaucrats, all sociologists (with a handful of exceptions), most economists (with growing exceptions), most conventional political scientists, almost all press education, health, housing and pension correspondents and most members of the public sector trade unions (p. 296).

Yet none of the four main components of the welfare state – education, health, housing, pensions – has to be transferred wholly to the state (pp. 296, 297). Indeed, many of the extensive functions that government has acquired over the past 130 years are not unavoidable collective functions, but are continued for no better reason than that the vested interests that supply them would be inconvenienced if they were transferred to the market (p. 299).

The tragedy is that although there often is another way – the market – government welfare has continued for so long that the possibility of other ways is far from the public mind. 'How else can hospitals be provided?' typifies the state of public knowledge that obstructs reform. The state has thus succeeded in the supreme aim of the monopolist – making itself seem indispensable (p. 302).

The British, however, are not inherently stupid. They would know what was meant if they were told in plain English that much of their intimate everyday personal and family lives has been the artificial creation of party politics and could be changed without injustice or hardship (p. 307).

They – especially those on lower incomes – do not have to suffer sink schools for their children; they do not have to wait months for varicose vein surgery nor years for hip replacement; they do not have to live in slum houses nor vandalised council tower blocks; they do not have to live in old age on a third of their earnings in work (p. 307).

These are all the creation of the state and its agencies. And the complaints, mainly from their employees, of underfunding are the familiar special pleading of vested interests. In fact, more money dispensed by the same people on the same principles would do little or nothing to change the mechanisms that produce the low standards, capricious quality and bureaucratic indifference of the welfare state (p. 307).

Nothing less will suffice than to change the status and power of the beneficiaries from grateful supplicants to demanding customers. That revolution in the status of the ordinary man and woman requires no more than a change from government monopoly to competition between suppliers in the market: the transformation of the artificial socialist welfare created by government to the development of the capitalist welfare that the people were creating for themselves in the nineteenth century (p. 307).

For the question, not asked by the politicians or academics lost in wonder at the welfare state, is what the people would be doing with their money today, without the taxation made necessary by our bloated welfare system. Their low incomes decades ago could have been supplemented to enable them to exercise the bargaining power of consumers in the competitive markets for welfare that were beginning to emerge (pp. 307, 308).

The stronger and wider demand for rising standards and choice in welfare would, as usual in the market, have evoked the faster response of increasing numbers of suppliers and kinds of schools, hospitals, homes and pensions-savings schemes (p. 308).

The politicians and academics, state school teachers and state-employed doctors evidently expect ordinary people to share their middle-class revulsion at the prospect of schools and hospitals being sold like baked beans or pea soup. Ordinary people may counter with the sad wish that schools and hospitals had been 'sold' at the high quality of the goods and services they pay for in the market (p. 308).

The time they began to get it right

Since World War II, hundreds of books and thousands of news-paper articles have portrayed the welfare state as the acme of compassion. Yet this view ignores the spontaneous antecedents to the services created by government. It ignores what were in fact the transitory reasons for the origins of state education in 1870, council housing in 1915 and 1919, state pensions in 1908 and 1925 and the NHS in 1948. And it denies experience in other countries with comparable cultures (p. 313).

A brief visit to the beginnings of welfare in the mid-1800s will reveal the middle-class myths about the callous self-neglect of our great-great-grandparents and show the shape that early capi-talist education, capitalist medical care, housing and pensions would have developed in the past decades if they had not been prevented by the state, its agencies, controllers and employees (p. 309).

For the much-derided 'Victorian values' taught responsibility, self-reliance, economy and integrity often absent from socialised activity, even under capitalism (p. 318).

Early promise in education

From the earliest years of the nineteenth century, and earlier, parents had begun to send their children to school. Their incomes were low; they required help, and received it from the Church, charitable and other sources. School fees, even only a few pence a week in the early years, might still require some sacrifice of the staples of food and clothing, but it was made (p. 315).

Parents, themselves largely illiterate, were increasingly anxious that their children should learn the elements of reading, writing and arithmetic. Education would have been among the earliest candidates for household budgeting after the staples of everyday life (p. 315).

Yet this is not the impression conveyed by the historians or the social novelists. The historians had drawn their evidence from official mid-nineteenth-century reports on the still large numbers who attended no school. Charles Dickens and the other social novelists had drawn for their fiction on the worst schools (p. 315).

It seems that then, as now, the failures, even if exceptional, excited more interest and sold more books than the successes. The normal was boring; the exceptional evoked philanthropic sympathy, literary imagination or political anger (p. 315).

Socialism has always thrived on hypothetical and apparently costless cures for painful symptoms. Private schools had failed to educate all children, therefore, some argued, the market must not supply education for anyone if some cannot pay for it. Their payment by taxes, originally indirect as well as later direct, is rarely discussed. That is a confusion between nationalising supply and fortifying demand (pp. 315, 316).

If demand is inadequate because some incomes are low, the logical solution is to top them up so that all parents can pay, not to create a state monopoly supply for everyone without much choice, little influence and less prospect of escape. Food and clothing are more elemental than education. That is not an argument for state monopolies (p. 316).

The number of children at pre-1870 private schools more than doubled from around 500,000 in 1818 to more than 1,250,000 in 1834. By 1851 two out of three were receiving daily instruction from the age of four or six until the age of ten. Professor Mark Blaug has concluded that by 1850 the rate of school attendance and literacy in England, in mainly parent-financed schools, exceeded that in the world as a whole in 1950, a century later (pp. 318, 319).

How much farther would parent-influenced unpoliticised schooling have spread if it had not been discouraged and repressed by the state? How many more parents today, with much higher incomes than their great-great-grandparents earned in 1870, especially if raised by lower indirect and direct taxes, would willingly be paying for the schools of their choice? We shall never know. The historians do not ask (p. 321).

The socialist mind shrinks from the question and is blind to the prospect. But the number must be many times the 7 per cent of children at such parent-financed schools of today. With earmarked school grants, or vouchers, virtually every working-class child could have the advantages of responsive schooling that treats parents as customers who pay, because they have the power to withdraw from bad schools as much as from bad restaurants (p. 321).

Clearly, there were bad private schools in the Victorian era, and the social novelists exploited them profitably in their fiction. But cases of bad specimens are not evidence against capitalism (nor cases of good state schools evidence for socialism). Bad schools would not have lasted long as purchasing power rose or was supplied by government to supplement low incomes. They need have lasted no longer than bad private restaurants (p. 322).

The private schools were spreading in a system that opened exits from bad suppliers; the state schools were created in a system that closed exits. Today, some 93 in each 100 parents are still prevented or inhibited from giving their children the schooling of their choice. That is the inhumanity of the political process (p. 322).

The beginnings of general medical care

Medical provision has fared no better. The spontaneous development of health services by the friendly societies, medical institutes, industrial insurance and other mechanisms of the nineteenth-century market – capitalist medicine – was hindered and finally almost destroyed by politicians, bureaucrats and producers in successive stages, culminating in the 1948 National Health Service – 'socialist medicine' (p. 323).

The embryonic medical market a century and more ago was developing consumer sovereignty; the NHS replaced it with producer dominance under the guise of political paternalism and professional benevolence. The evolving buyers' market, in which the consumers employed the doctors who danced to their tune, was followed by the state-enforced sellers' market, in which the consumers became supplicants in the doctors' surgery (p. 323).

This sorry tale, in essentials disguised by political claims to create equality, justice and compassion, is the economic history of British medicine. Over the century, socialist thinking has prevailed over liberal teaching on the consequences, in all human behaviour, of state coercion, concentration of power, monopoly and producer myopia (p. 323).

British health services will not improve radically until the sellers' market of the NHS yields to a buyers' market. NHS waiting and queuing, by patients for doctors, will have to be reversed. Doctors will have to wait for patients (p. 323).

The difference is that the long waiting of patients in the NHS – often weeks for consultations, months for some surgery and years for so-called non-urgent surgery that causes mental anxiety and often physical deterioration – could be replaced by short occasional waiting by doctors. This is because the market is so much more efficient in coordinating the time of individual patients and doctors than are the centralised procedures of the state (p. 323).

The NHS was politically sold to the electorate with the promise that everyone would have the best medical care that science could produce. This echo of the lofty Marxist promise '... to each according to his needs ...' was a deception for which democracy, the doctors and the people are still suffering (p. 324).

It has degraded political democracy into a political auction, misled the doctors into thinking that government could isolate healthcare from the fundamental human condition of scarcity, and callously aroused unfulfillable expectations of universal medical care without limit of cost in doctors' time, hospital equipment, ambulance facilities and innumerable other scarce resources that civilised society must husband scrupulously or lose in a scramble for survival (p. 324).

Yet these principles of care and economy in the use of resources were being respected by the working men of England and being incorporated into their early efforts to build medical services for themselves and their families in the nineteenth century. The spontaneous arrangements made by them with doctors in medical institutes, clubs and other organisations would not have misled the people, the doctors or politicians into unrealisable expectations (p. 324).

The capitalist idea faced reality and produced solutions to maximise the good that could be extracted from scarce resources. The socialist idea in the NHS unthinkingly begged all the questions that face humanity by applying the naivety of the central Marxist fallacy of the relationship between human nature and scarce resources (p. 324).

The Great Western Railway Medical Fund Society of Swindon,

established in 1847, a century before the NHS, had by 1944 employed fourteen full-time doctors and consultants, and three full-time dentists. It ran a 42-bed hospital with a large outpatients' department caring for over 40,000 members and their families, half the population of Swindon. The Llanelli and District Medical Service had 18,000 subscribers in 1937 to its comprehensive 'model of any national system of medical services' (p. 326).

Swindon and Llanelli were not unique. That they were not untypical is indicated by the fact that the number of medical institutes rose from two in 1870 to 32 in 1883, with 139,000 members, and to 85 in 1910, with 329,000 members (p. 326).

Then came compulsory insurance for sickness cash grants in 1911. It played havoc with self-help. Despite increasing numbers of potential members, the number of medical institutes fell from 88 in 1912, with 312,000 members, to 49 in 1947, with 166,000 members. Then came the NHS in 1948. It seemed to sound the death knell for self-help through voluntary medical insurance. All the medical institutes had closed by 1949 (p. 326).

The warning of the nineteenth-century Whig statesman Henry Brougham, on schools, was vindicated in medicine: '… it behoves us to take the greatest care how we interfere with a system which prospers so well'. The market then was doing its work in medicine as in education (p. 327).

But the political process has propulsions other than those of putting the individual in command of his destiny. Of the 12 million coerced into state insurance by the 1911 Act, 9 million had already been covered by voluntary schemes – in registered and unregistered societies. Membership had been growing at accelerating rates for a third of a century. The 2.8 million in registered societies, in 1877, had risen by 90,000 a year to 3.6 million in 1887, then by 120,000 a year to 4.8 million in 1897 and again by 140,000 to 6.6 million by 1910 (p. 327).

At the same rate of acceleration, a million more in all schemes would have been covered by the time of the 1914 war. All this was destroyed, not by the will of the people, but by the political process. The familiar pretexts of more rapid state action, widespread poverty and the untidy patchwork quilt of care concealed less worthy motives of party political advantage, bureaucratic empire-building and capitulation to organised interests (p. 327).

Yet the market, despite suppression by government, recovered by the forces of supply and demand. After World War II, voluntary health insurance through the remnants of the friendly societies recovered and resumed its methods of payment for medicine in the market (p. 327).

The gradual growth in demand came from heads of families with rising incomes and from employers who wanted prompter and better medical attention for employees whom they were anxious not to lose when it suited the NHS – which said, in effect, 'Don't call us, we'll call you.' The NHS illustrates the consequences of taking a service from the market and putting it into the political process (p. 327).

The market process, in which the scores of Llanelli Medical Institutes and Great Western Railway Societies enabled the miner, the railwayman, the steelworker, the weaver, the tailor and cobbler to decide their lives, was almost destroyed. The political process into which the socialist mind propelled them by compulsory insurance and taxation was not a substitute for the consumer sovereignty of the market but its destroyer (p. 328).

The NHS is not the envy of the world, as its uncritical supporters claimed. Only Italy copied it systematically in 1981, and it came to grief in two or three years. New Zealand's gradually developing state structure suffers much the same distortions as the NHS. The British attempt at socialised medicine has been a cul-de-sac that, like state education, threatened working-class subjection, from which the increasingly affluent workers are escaping only by the rising living standards provided by capitalism (p. 329).

Today, when the British could be savouring consumer sovereignty in medicine, their politicians are still having to make concessions to producer dominance. That is the reality of the political process (p. 330).

Self-help in housing

Few academics, of the left or right, would now claim that the political process has provided the British with the homes they prefer. Whether they wish to own or rent, many have not been able to live as they wish for over 70 years. They have been prevented by two understandable but in the event disastrous political decisions (p. 330).

In 1915, the wartime government restricted home rents with the plausible intention of keeping housing costs down and discouraging inflationary wage demands, which would have complicated the financing of the war. In 1919, the government required local authorities to build houses to let at subsidised rents for the further plausible reason that the rent restrictions had reduced to a trickle the spontaneous growth in home ownership and discouraged private investment in building homes for renting (p. 330).

The result by the 1970s was to put more than 6 million working-class families into council housing or tower blocks that they would not have chosen for themselves. This political artefact amounted to one third of the total housing stock. That was a source of pride to doctrinaire Labour and unreflecting Conservative politicians (p. 330).

Yet their legacy comprises the physical deterioration of council homes, streets and districts, the tower blocks that made millions of working men accept a window-box in place of a garden and their wives the risk of a mugger as well as a burglar, not least the denial of the opportunity of owning a home to build a nest-egg of savings for their old age (p. 330).

It also includes yet one more example of the government failure that can neither acknowledge error nor redeem it expeditiously. Although Mrs Thatcher's governments had by the early 1990s sold over a million council homes to their tenants, the political process in housing has grown barnacles of vested interests that will continue the myth of council housing benevolence well into the 21st century (p. 331).

The market would have reacted promptly to a change in social conditions. It would have pulled down the council houses of the 1950s, 1960s and 1970s, and replaced them with homes that the increasing numbers of affluent workers actually wanted. Instead, the political process will consign millions of the working classes to council homes for many years to come (p. 331).

The socialist vision, at its best in intention, was Aneurin Bevan's mixed council estates for middle-class and working-class tenants to encourage social integration. But this made the characteristic socialist mistake of ignoring the gradual enrichment of capitalism (p. 331).

The workers were becoming middle-class faster than the politicians could see, and their children – with two cars, two televisions and two holidays a year – would not tolerate the slums built by the state. They did not require paternalistic politicians to tell them where and how to live. They would have been better served by the capitalist vision of a free market in which they could buy or rent the homes they preferred (p. 331).

Yet the market had been emerging for over a century. The stock of privately-built, low-cost homes (including shops with flats) rose from 3.9 million in 1875 to 6.4 million in 1910. Few academic studies have asked how much further the number would have grown if the state had supplied housing grants instead of cheap housing that made the tenants the submissive importunates of council officials from whom only some two in five or six have so far escaped (updated estimate) (p. 331).

The shabby housing of the working poor was a common complaint of the official reports and unofficial novels of the nine-teenth century. But this view often overlooked the improvements that rising incomes were already bringing with capitalist invest-ment in housing (p. 332).

In 1871, the Royal Commission on Friendly and Benefit Building Societies was surprised to be told that 13,000 Birmingham working men owned their homes, and were buying them out of average wages of some £1.50 a week. In 1884, the Royal Commission on Housing learned that the Leeds Permanent Benefit Building Society had enabled 7,000 working men to buy their homes (p. 332).

It cannot be supposed that Birmingham and Leeds were the only industrial towns in which home ownership was spreading. Some of the commissioners were sceptical and surprised. But the market did not publicise itself as did government. And the social historians did not dig deeply for the evidence of self-help in housing; the surmise must be that they did not expect to find it (p. 332).

Nor did self-help in housing develop only in the towns. Samuel Smiles, the once-reviled author of *Self-Help* (1859), wrote in a later book, *Thrift*, published in 1875: 'There are exceptional towns and villages in Lancashire where large sums have been saved by the operatives for buying or building comfortable cottage dwellings. The Burnley Building Society ... has 6,600 investors ... principally mill operatives, miners, mechanics, engineers, carpenters, stonemasons, and labourers. They include women, both married and unmarried' (p. 332).

Certainly, if government had since helped emerging workers to independence, instead of tying them to the state, some 3 million (updated figure) British families would not still be living in council homes that they would not have chosen and cannot adapt to their liking. The dreary council houses and the Soviet-like tower blocks, which house crime, would have been unknown (p. 333).

The great pensions 'con'

Pensions too are likely to have been in far better shape if the state had helped the spontaneous saving institutions instead of making its coercive takeover bid by establishing the political fraud of national insurance. It began well in 1908 with the Liberal pensions of 50p a week for people of 70 years with little or no other income (p. 334).

But in 1925 the Conservative government of Stanley Baldwin succumbed to the political temptation to spread its wings, acquire a new device for winning the affection of voters and create a new source of government revenue (p. 334).

The politicians ignored the inconvenient warning that the liberal economist Alfred Marshall had given to the 1893 Royal

Commission on the Aged Poor: 'Universal pensions ... do not contain ... the seeds of their own disappearance. I am afraid that, if started, they would tend to become perpetual' (p. 334).

Sadly, the political process induces even the most upright of politicians to take the short view. The Royal Commission did not devise a pension that would 'disappear' with poverty among the aged. The state pension, nominally based on a national insurance invested fund, but in truth largely financed by current taxes, is now paid to some 11 million (updated figure) pensioners among whom poverty is vanishing (p. 334).

But the machinery of politics moves like an oil tanker. It pays the politicians to continue presenting 'the pensioners' as poor and pathetic. That is the humanity and compassion of the political process (p. 334).

State pensions have thus become not only perpetual, but have been self-expanding, a discouragement to labour mobility, a confidence trick on the pensioner (they are not guaranteed by insurance), a further corruption of representative government and a vast and still growing liability on the national exchequer (p. 334).

The system rests on the irony that it grows as national and personal incomes grow. The notion that, as the nation becomes richer, it can afford higher state pensions is a confusion of thought in welfare state politics. As the national income rises, so do personal incomes. The state is then supposed to distribute higher pensions as the people who retire require less. The result is that the state pension is paid to the increasingly affluent (p. 334).

In his survey *Welfare before the Welfare State*, the academic Dr Charles Hanson documented the spontaneous self-help in saving for old age in the nineteenth century and exposed several works by academics for understating the massive growth of voluntary insurance. He himself concluded that by the early twentieth century the proportion of men not voluntarily insured against sickness, and thus to some extent against old age, was 'a small minority' (pp. 335, 336).

In this way, the British showed themselves to be neither feckless nor callous. They had cared for their families. If the state had not taken part of their earnings, first by indirect and then by direct taxes to pay for compulsory benefits, they would have done more. And they were caring more as their income rose (p. 336).

Research for examination of the Crossman proposals for 'National Superannuation' in 1956 (another political euphemism for compulsory social benefits) revealed that the ordinary people had amassed several billions of savings in National Savings, building society shares, industrial and provident societies, friendly societies, industrial assurance, life assurance, homes, household goods and other property (p. 336).

Private pensions grew with the expansion of occupational pension schemes in the 1950s and 1960s. The first scheme had come in 1931. By 1936 membership had risen to 1.8 million, and by 1951 to 3.9 million in private industry. By the 1970s the total membership in funded schemes in industry and local government was around 12 million, increasingly of wage-paid as well as salaried employees (p. 336).

This movement emerged in the market. The capitalist employers were falling over themselves to attract staff by adding pensions as deferred pay to current pay (p. 336).

Predictably, the critics fastened on the defects: not all wage-earners, especially women and short-term workers, were covered (true, but improving); mobility was impeded (true, but remediable); the insurance companies were controlling the investment of the funds in industry (would a state monopoly have been preferable?); not least, the occupational pensions created two nations in old age (true, but the culprit was government for enforcing saving for retirement through social insurance). Again, the market effect was overlooked: private pensions made the workers independent of the political process and its questionable devices (p. 336).

Decades after the 1908 and 1925 pensions, the people who could be saving for early or late retirement in numerous ways are still having to contribute as taxpayers to a non-existent national insurance fund for a basic pension paid increasingly to the rich. The irony of the political process is that even where it sets out to do good it ends by doing harm (p. 337).

The story of pensions is thus essentially that of education, medicine and housing: the state jumped on all four of them and slowed them down (pp. 336, 337).

Self-reliance refuses to die

It may seem more difficult to rescue welfare from the political process than other goods and services that government has captured because the elector seems superficially fearful of letting go of nurse for fear of something worse. Yet it is also easier for the more fundamental reason that all four components were developed before the welfare state almost suppressed them (p. 337).

Their roots lie in the British character: its innate independence, its pride in self-help and its sense of responsibility for family. All have been weakened by the state, which usurped the role of parents, cut the bonds of sympathy between parents and children and incited all to look for succour and sustenance to officialdom.

Far from the market being too long absent to be restored, it is still in fact not far below the surface (p. 337).

The proven ability of the British to handle money was the legacy of the very market institutions in education, medicine and housing that the welfare state almost destroyed. The British had been providing cash benefits for themselves in sickness, unemployment and old age long before the state made its takeover bid for their voluntary institutions (pp. 339, 340).

They were elbowed out by politicians and bureaucrats who took their money, called taxes, to buy their assets, indulged in the strong-arm tactics of driving them out of the market by charging less than cost (the euphemism of 'free') and continually threatened them with extinction (p. 340).

There can be no remaining doubt that the bulk of the state services in kind could gradually have been replaced by cash, certainly from the 1920s. The welfare state created after World War II at the end of the 1940s could then have been avoided by refinement of methods to top up the lower incomes (p. 340).

All the people, including even the physically disabled and except only the mentally sick, could then have taken their place as consumers shopping for education, medicine, housing and pensions together with the increasing majority whose earnings required no topping up. That is the capitalist vision of welfare in the market (p. 340).

There is, of course, the danger of the debilitating effect on character of unearned income from the state, the risk that it would be misspent and the uncertainty whether many parents can be entrusted with the interests of their children. But money is superior to services because it is only by human experience that error can be learned and avoided. And even if not all learn to avoid error, there is no reason to subject those who do to the same paternalism (p. 340).

When the people can choose in the market process, with realistic calculation of individual costs and benefits, they will choose private rather than state education, private doctors and hospitals rather than the NHS, buying or renting homes of their choice rather than paying even subsidised rents in council tenantry and private, flexible and transferable rather than standardised and politicised state pensions (p. 341).

Beware monopoly

There is the serious charge against capitalism of inefficiency, because of monopoly and restrictive practices. This is partly true, but also partly untrue because much, if not most, monopoly would not persist without government support. A high degree of monopoly is unavoidable, at least for a time, possibly for some years, exceptionally for decades, where large firms can produce at lower costs than small firms (p. 254).

But it is more easily corrected than in socialism, as capitalism has developed a structure of anti-monopoly 'trust-busting' laws. These may on balance, at times, do less good in disciplining monopoly than harm in weakening the internal organic reaction of firms to changes in markets. For obsessive 'fussing' about the imperfections of markets – like the hypochondriac who reacts to every change of body temperature – has produced cures that may be worse than the disease (p. 254).

But socialism enthrones monopoly as an instrument of government. It is called by other names – 'public ownership' or 'social ownership' – but it replaces what could have been a choice of several or many private competing suppliers by one dominant public or social supplier. The virtue of the market is that the consumer can compare alternative goods and services and test them by trial (pp. 254, 255).

In fact, new technology – and the replacement of mass-production heavy industry by medium-sized and small firms – is likely to be a powerful and continuing force for undermining concentrations of private industry in monopolies, cartels and restrictive agreements (p. 423).

More power to women

Another reason for optimism about the future of liberal capitalism is the emergent influence of women in all walks of life, political as well as economic. In the political process their influence may not be that different from that of men – although they are less accustomed to the herd instinct of political life and therefore more likely to rebel as individuals than acquiesce in its majoritarian procedures (p. 420).

But in the economic world the influence of women will be very different. Broadly, men in industry are still inclined to delegate market bargaining to industrial, professional and trade union organisations that produce collective decisions by majorities of the activists (p. 420).

Women are more characteristically makers of individual decisions in the market. The division of labour so far has allotted them the function of purchasing consumer for household supplies. The archetypal family has been headed by the earning male and the spending female (p. 420).

Even where women work and earn, they retain the main

function of shopper and consumer – even when shopping with males. Men are more characteristically political animals and women domestic. The more women that work and earn, the stronger will be their influence in household budgeting. The increasing influence of women as shoppers and consumers, relative to that of men, will hopefully induce and fortify government to withstand the importunities of organised producers (p. 420).

An aid to world peace

Overall, a world of capitalist countries which minimises the domain of government and maximises the activities of men and women in the market, at home and overseas, is more likely to keep the peace than a world of socialist states. This is because it is more likely to create an international market in which individuals and private firms rather than governments, traders rather than politicians, do business with each other. The much-maligned multinational companies are thus by definition vested interests in favour of world peace (p. 383).

The critics of global capitalism condemn its commercialisation of human activities. But if capitalism is replaced by socialism, the market process and its commercialisation, with its higher living standards and strengths and weaknesses, will be replaced by the political process and by politicisation, with its more doubtful strengths and less removable weaknesses (p. 402).

That is the alternative. There can be no doubt which is preferable. The market process allows decisions to be made by individuals for themselves; the political process requires them to be made by collectives and imposed on individuals and minorities. The market process aggrandises the individual; he may be wrong, but his decision decides. The political process suppresses the individual in collective decisions (p. 402).

Capitalism must be judged not only by what it has achieved, despite its shortcomings, but even more by what it could achieve if the political process were corralled to its essentials and refined much more than it has been so far to reflect the microeconomic preferences as well as the macroeconomic opinions of the citizenry (p. 426).

Capitalism: not perfect – but our best hope

The prospects for capitalism in general are bright. But the living standards of the West are still restrained and unnecessarily unequal because the political process has too many beneficiaries in all political parties (p. 434).

Capitalism has never been and never will be faultless. But it can remove many of its imperfections. The socialist alternative of incorporating the market as a subordinate instrument of the state is little more than one more attempt to salvage the socialist vision. Yet if the fate of ordinary people is their concern, socialist thinkers can help them most by joining the task of fashioning a less imperfect capitalism (pp. 430, 431)

Some socialist thinkers have abandoned socialism to the extent of understanding and accepting markets. Many remain faithful to the socialist dream of the beneficence of the saints and seers they see as forming governments. The rest of the world must leave them to their dreams while it refines the imperfect instruments developed in capitalism for providing mankind with an increasingly tolerable and civilised world (pp. 433, 434).

3   CAPITALISM GOOD, SOCIALISM BAD
James Bartholomew[1]

The culture of anti-capitalism

How did 'capitalism' become a dirty word? Hostility has slipped in, unopposed, and become pervasive.

It has even reached sport. Last year [2006], a correspondent on Radio 4's *Today* programme reported on a proposal coming from the European Union to put a cap on the salaries of footballers. He treated this as though it were probably a good thing. Not the merest hint was there that this was interference with a market and therefore likely – like most interferences in markets – to have unintended, damaging effects.

The Church of England joined in the anti-capitalist *zeitgeist* with particular enthusiasm the same week. It issued a report called *Faithful Cities* in which it questioned 'our reliance on market driven capitalism'. The report referred to how capitalism 'promotes inequality'. The authors felt no need to provide evidence for this assertion. They just took it as read. The report went on to say that

---

1   James Bartholomew is an author and journalist. He was a leader writer on the *Daily Telegraph* and the *Daily Mail* and continues to write for these publications, as well as the *Mail on Sunday*, the *Sunday Telegraph* and the *Spectator*, on a freelance basis. He is the author of *The Richest Man in the World: The Sultan of Brunei* (1989), *Yew and Non-Yew* (1998) and, most recently, *The Welfare State We're In* (2004) – a detailed and rigorous analysis of the impact of the welfare state on British society.

the gap between the rich and those 'in poverty' should be reduced. So in the Church's eyes, capitalism produces inequality and this inequality is bad. It is hard to conclude anything other than that the Church of England now regards capitalism as bad.

We need a culture check here. A society that widely regards capitalism as bad will, in due course, destroy it. Incredibly, it seems necessary to assert afresh that capitalism is the goose that lays the golden eggs – the foundation of the extraordinary wealth we now enjoy compared to all previous eras of world history.

I was going to say, 'Let's take a revision course in why capitalism is good.' But few of us had an initial lesson. I don't suggest that every school should have been teaching the virtues of capitalism but right now they do precisely the opposite. They teach that capitalists destroy rainforests, control American foreign policy and spread the human vices of greed and selfishness. Anti-capitalism is now the subtext of history and geography lessons, as well politics, economics and sociology. Capitalism is said to have given rise to slavery. The state is depicted as a hero that has tempered the cruelty of the beast with laws, regulations and interventions. If you have children at school – state or private, it doesn't make any difference – he or she gets another little dose of anti-capitalist propaganda every day. It is all absurdly lopsided, of course, and it puts our society on a self-destructive path.

The achievements of capitalism

What is the biggest benefit that the relatively poor have experienced over the past two centuries? It is surely the terrific reduction in the relative cost of food. Two centuries ago, the cost of food was the biggest element in a family's budget. It was hard for a poor family to get enough to eat. If there was a shortage, there could be a famine, resulting in thousands of deaths. Even in the shorter period since the 1920s, average spending on food has fallen from a third of average incomes to only a tenth. The cost of food has plummeted. Look at any chart of the price of the basic foodstuffs like wheat, barley and milk and you will see almost continuous and deep falls. What has caused this massive benefit to the poor? A series of government regulations? A good-looking politician with an easy smile and a 'vision'? No. Capitalism.

No single individual did it. Thousands, or millions, did it. They were not directed by any central agency. They just operated in a capitalist system. They invented farm machinery that replaced many men and therefore made food much cheaper. Farmers deployed these machines. Others created ships that could carry grain cheaply, quickly and in great volume from faraway lands where food was grown more cheaply. Others still distributed the food in ever more cost-efficient ways, by rail and by road on newly created and deployed trains and lorries. They did this, each of them living their own separate lives in their own undirected ways. They transformed the situation. The poor were given food in abundance. They were given it at a price they could easily afford. Shortages, hunger and famine became history. That is what capitalism did. To sneer at it is to sneer at the abolition of hunger in this country.

This has been, perhaps, capitalism's greatest achievement. But that is just one of many benefits it has provided. Capitalism achieved a similar feat in clothing. Two centuries ago, many people had clogs on their feet. Clothing was another major expense for the poor. Nye Bevan, as a child, threw an inkwell at his teacher because the man made fun of a boy whose family could afford only one pair of shoes between the boy and his brother. That is a measure of the poverty that we have come from. That is the poverty from which capitalism has elevated this country. Again, new and much cheaper methods of production have been put in place by individuals importing cotton, improving textile production techniques, deploying new kinds of transport and distributing the raw material and final products more cheaply. No longer do children share shoes. Capitalism has done this.

Capitalism has made us richer and given us the opportunity of vastly more diverse experiences. Even in my own lifetime, I have seen the normal length of holidays rise from one or two weeks to four or five weeks. Foreign travel that was completely unknown for the vast majority of working people two centuries ago is now commonplace. Did government direction make this possible? Of course not.

Most families now have cars. Read Thomas Hardy's novels and you find that people are always walking in them. Of course, walking can be healthy and pleasant. But the average family of Hardy's time did not have any choice.

Who invented cars? Who built them? Who refined their design and manufacture to the point where they can be afforded by millions of people? Not governments. The diverse, resourceful power of capitalism.

Why does the system work? Because it provides incentives and motivation. If you invent something new, you may get fame and fortune. If you supply food, clothes or cars more cheaply than the next person, you get more customers. Simple enough. Provide a good product or service at a low price and you have a business. That simple logic means capitalism tends to produce good products and services at better prices.

Capitalism and inequality

What about the argument that capitalism promotes inequality? Let's remember, before starting to answer, just how disastrous were the attempts in the twentieth century to impose equality. Farmers in Stalinist Russia were prosecuted and in many cases killed during the appalling 'collectivisation' of farms in which small individual farms were forced to combine into big communal ones. Tens of millions died under communist rule in China. And after all the oppression and suffering, there was still no equality in those countries. There was the privileged ruling class with, in Russia's case, special dachas in the country and road lanes in town. Imposing equality is not an easy ride. It is an oppressive one and doomed to failure.

But capitalism has claims, at least, to reducing inequality over time. The inequality was enormous when George III was sitting on his gilded throne in 1806 with thousands of servants, farm workers and other underlings at his beck and call while, elsewhere in the country, there were people who could barely find enough to eat and, in some cases, who died of hunger. Nowadays, over nine out of ten youths have mobile phones; 99 per cent of households have colour televisions; most households have cars. Yes, the rich are still with us. But the contrast in financial wealth has been greatly reduced over the long term. That was not due to any government, let alone a deliberate attempt to promote equality. It was achieved by capitalism.

The welfare state

It is said by some politicians in all the parties, 'Yes, capitalism has its uses. But on the other hand, the state is the natural and best provider of welfare. We should combine capitalism with government-provided welfare.'

This is to turn a blind eye to how disastrously bad the state has been at providing welfare. In healthcare, one of the more objective measures is the proportion of people who survive for five years after being diagnosed with one of the various forms of cancer. For most of the major cancers, Britain has one of the worst records, or perhaps the worst record, in western Europe. In breast cancer, for example, Britain has the worst five-year survival rates among advanced European countries. A woman diagnosed with breast cancer in Britain is 40 per cent more likely to die within five years than a woman in France. Professor Karol Sikora has calculated that the treatment provided by the National Health Service (NHS) has resulted in 10,000 people a year dying of cancer who would not have died if Britain was of an average standard among western European countries. Britain has had the most state-controlled healthcare system in the advanced world and – by many measures – has had the worst. Many have suffered and died unnecessarily as a result.

Of course, it is now said that things will get better. More money is being collected in taxes and put into the NHS. Hopes and excuses are always abundant when politicians talk about the NHS. They always have been, ever since it was created in 1948. But over that long time, the hope of a first-class, state-run service has not been fulfilled. The excuses have had to become cleverer and more improbable. A great experiment is currently under way to see whether lots more money will bring the NHS up to the average European standard. The early evidence – from the low take-up of new, improved cancer drugs, to take just one example – is that it will not.

As for education, the single most damning piece of evidence of government failure comes from the government itself. In one of its own surveys, it found that the rate of adult functional illiteracy in Britain is 20 per cent. That is after over 80 years of free, compulsory primary education.

Government welfare was created, in many cases, with good intentions. But it has disappointed and its failure goes beyond providing healthcare and education of a patchy and often low standard. Government welfare has also done great, unintended damage to British society.

It has created mass unemployment on a permanent basis. Of course, unemployment existed prior to state welfare. But it was only in the wake of the 1911 National Insurance Act that we came to have so much unemployment on a permanent basis. One should include, for this purpose, not only the officially unemployed but, as the government itself now admits, at least a million of those who receive incapacity benefit. There are many others, too, who should rightly be classified as unemployed. Unemployment is still appallingly widespread. This is damaging to those who suffer it and to society more generally. Those directly affected are severely demoralised. Many find themselves strongly incentivised not to be honest. The cost of the benefits results in higher taxes for everyone else, which, incidentally, then go on to cause yet more unemployment.

The cost of the welfare state is now the major cost of government and has made government permanently very expensive. This has led to the taxation of people whom the government itself defines as being in 'poverty'. The economic growth of Britain has been held back. Without the cost of the modern welfare state, using an OECD analysis, the economic growth generated by lower taxation would have caused the British people to be among the richest in the world.

The unintended, unexpected damage done by state welfare includes the vast increase in unmarried parenting and the appalling rise in the level of crime – particularly violent crime. Mass unemployment, children being brought up without their fathers, fathers without responsibility for families, dependency on the government for everything, sink estates and sink schools, these have all contributed to the rise in crime. From being an outstandingly peaceful, law-abiding nation from Edwardian times up until the 1950s and 1960s, Britain has descended to a level of incivility and criminality that is among the worst in the advanced world. There is no sign, either, that this trend has reached its end.

Welfare provision without the state

Could capitalism have done better? Well, it is not just capitalism which was the alternative – at least not capitalism as it is normally understood. Prior to the modern welfare state, there was an unorganised mixture of welfare provision – as unorganised as the massive reduction in food prices. It started with self-help and went on through family welfare and mutual help through a wide variety of institutions, especially friendly societies, and welfare provision in its commercial forms. If none of this worked or was sufficient, there was a vast amount of charitable or semi-charitable welfare.

This enormously diverse non-state welfare included all the leading teaching hospitals of London. It included virtually all the most famous provincial hospitals, among them the Radcliffe Infirmary in Oxford, where the first person in the world received treatment with what was immediately called 'the miracle drug':

penicillin. Penicillin was probably the greatest single medical advance of the twentieth century. It was developed by the British medical profession in combination with various charitable foundations and commercial ventures prior to the creation of the NHS.

Britain had a healthcare system, prior to the NHS, which even the Labour Party, in suggesting a National Service for Health in 1942, found hard to criticise. It provided far more hospital beds and hospitals than now exist. The NHS has closed down medical capacity, not increased it.

In education, again there was an extraordinary mixture of provision before the state established a monopoly. But the most remarkable thing about it, as Arthur Seldon emphasises in *Capitalism*, is how it was advancing. During the first three-quarters of the nineteenth century, with minimal government involvement, the provision of schooling raced away. David Lloyd George received an excellent education at an Anglican church in a remote part of western Wales. It is doubtful whether the son of an artisanal family in such a place today would receive anything like as good an education as he did. He was reading the great historians Gibbon and Macaulay before he left school at fourteen.

Most important of all, non-state social security provision did not have the hugely damaging effects of state welfare. The vast majority of male industrial workers were members of friendly societies. These now widely forgotten institutions provided mutual help. The members paid regular contributions and were covered against a variety of possible disasters. The troubles that were covered varied from one society to another. They could include insurance against unemployment or sickness. They could offer a benefit to a widow if her husband died. They could offer medical insurance and, towards the end of the century, they began to offer pensions. Trade unions also provided some similar welfare provisions. All this was growing and developing rapidly. It would be perverse to think that it would not have continued to grow and develop if the state had not taken over.

Why is capitalism now so widely despised? Why is state welfare considered inevitable, if not actually good?

The collapse of communism

As far as capitalism is concerned, the collapse of the communist states in the late twentieth century removed from our sight useful reminders of how vastly superior capitalism is to state control. Is that why our culture is gradually forgetting capitalism's value?

From the end of World War II until 1989, when the Berlin Wall came down, newspapers regularly reported on the failings of communist countries. Of course, they had their defenders, but these gradually dwindled in number. The evidence became overwhelming that communism had been a terrible failure economically and had resulted in political oppression on a scale unprecedented in world history. Those on welfare benefits in the former West Germany were better off than those on the average wage in communist East Germany. As capitalist South Korea enjoyed outstanding economic growth, across the border in communist North Korea thousands were starving to death. When Russia gave up communism, we discovered even more about how basic and inferior was its healthcare provision.

Those of us who travelled in communist countries before the collapse could be in no doubt about the abject failure of communism – which is, after all, the antithesis to capitalism and the ultimate in state control. For myself, I will never forget seeing a 'supermarket' in Bucharest in 1982. The large container for refrigerated food was almost entirely empty. The only food in it was tinned and the container was not, in fact, refrigerated at all. In Irkutsk, in Siberia, I looked around the town for fresh fruit. I was keen to have some after several days without obtaining any. All I could find was one or two dried-out lemons.

Against that sort of background, it was easy to believe that capitalism was a far better system than communism and that personal freedom was an important part of its superiority. The residents of the communist countries were extremely restricted in their travel, in what they said and in every other aspect of their lives. I invited a man I met in Irkutsk to have supper with me. Soon after we sat down, a waitress came to him and told him there were some men who wanted to speak to him. He got up and I never saw him again. I have no doubt he was arrested and examined by the police for talking to a foreigner.

Now, though, with the almost total disappearance of communist states, the idea that capitalism itself is a poor system has become more widespread. Any suffering or inequality is highlighted and treated as symptomatic of failure. Understanding of the great superiority of capitalism to its alternatives has been slipping away. The complacency of many believers in free markets in 1989 and in the following few years has proved misplaced.

A neo-socialist future?

The idea that government should control things and put all wrongs right has become more powerful again since that time. The virtues of capitalism have been gradually forgotten. Not enough people are prepared to argue for them.

The problem is that, in a democracy, it is extremely tempting for politicians to win votes by promising that, under their control, the government will offer something for 'free'. It will put problems right. It is much more difficult for a politician to win votes by saying, 'The trouble with our society is that the government is doing too much.'

The people are sovereign and the only chance we have of holding on to the advantages of capitalism or rolling back the extent of state control is by persuading people of the virtues of capitalism. It is not an easy job. Nor is it a job that can be done once and for all. It is work that will need to be done in every generation. It is work that, ideally, would result in allowing, at least, the pro-capitalist case to be made in schools and universities. At present, school libraries tend to have plenty of books by Marx and Engels but very few by Friedrich Hayek, Milton Friedman or Adam Smith. Indeed, many teachers have not even heard of several of these important thinkers.

We do not need to ask for pro-capitalist propaganda. But we can reasonably ask that the pro-socialist propaganda be ended. We can argue that true education does not consist of putting only one side of an argument – an argument that is likely to last for many centuries.

We should be careful. If the demonisation of capitalism continues much longer, the goose that lays the golden eggs will be killed. We will not reap new and as yet undefined benefits that capitalism has yet to offer. The damaging economic, political and social effects of neo-socialism will become more and more serious.

4 WHY CAPITALISM MIGHT NOT SURVIVE
D. R. Myddelton[1]

The market system

Schumpeter famously asked [in 1943]: 'Can capitalism survive?'
His answer was: 'No. I do not think it can' (Schumpeter, 1954:
61–167). He took 100 pages to explain his reasons, which boiled
down to arguing that its very success would undermine the social
institutions that protect it. In other words, people would come to
take it for granted. What, then, are capitalism's essential features,
and what might weaken or destroy them?

Capitalism is sometimes known as 'private enterprise', but
I prefer to call it the 'market system'. Its essential features are
that individuals own personal property; they can earn income
by voluntary working under legally enforceable contracts; and
they can choose how to spend or save their money. Potential
producers are free to start up, merge or sell businesses and
compete with existing firms. There is a generally accepted

---

1   D. R. Myddelton was educated at Eton and the Harvard Business School. He is a
     chartered accountant. He was Professor of Finance and Accounting at the Cran-
     field School of Management from 1972 to 2005. For many years he has been a
     member of the Council of the University of Buckingham. He is also chairman of
     the managing trustees of the Institute of Economic Affairs. Professor Myddelton
     has written many books and articles on the subjects of tax and inflation, includ-
     ing *On a Cloth Untrue: Inflation Accounting, the Way Forward* (1984), *The Power to
     Destroy: A Study of the British Tax System* (2nd edn, 1994) and *Unshackling Account-
     ants* (2004).

medium of exchange (money) with a reasonably stable purchasing power over time.

Both Schumpeter and Arthur Seldon contrasted capitalism with socialism; but I suggest the alternative to the market system is the 'political system' (or simply 'politics'). This can obstruct the market in many ways. It may conscript people against their will to fight in a war. It may debase the (state monopoly) currency, which distorts price signals and estimates of business profit or loss. It may restrict property rights by foreign exchange controls which prevent imports of goods or travelling abroad.

Politics and the law

Politics may pervert the 'law'. As Alan Bullock said of Hitler: '[He] never abandoned the cloak of legality: he recognised the enormous psychological value of having the law on his side. Instead he turned the law inside out and made illegality legal' (Bullock, 1962: 257). An example is penal retrospective legislation. Some years ago the Leasehold Reform Act deprived landlords of some of their rights in this way; but since landlords were just an unpopular minority most people neither noticed nor cared. Hardly any lawyers objected on principle, yet each new retrospective 'law' further undermines the rule of law.

Another example was the War Damage Act. After the war, this changed the law back to what a government spokesman claimed 'everyone had always thought it was'. That 'everyone' did not include the highest court in the land. But a mere court was not allowed to stand in the government's way. Indeed, a minister even asserted: 'It is our responsibility and duty to override the court where we think that it is a proper and just thing to do.' This was an explicit end to any lingering notion of *limited* government under the rule of law.

Almost every Finance Act nowadays contains retrospective 'laws'. Modern British governments observe the law only when they choose: they regard themselves as above the law. Herbert Spencer said: 'The divine right of kings has become the divine right of parliaments.' An especially outrageous recent 'law' purports to make it illegal for English people to refer in business dealings to certain non-metric measures.

Governments sometimes use the law to threaten some all-purpose foe such as 'terrorists'. They may pass a very fierce law which, by concession, is not always fully enforced: for example, imprisoning terrorist suspects without charge for up to 28 days (the government wanted 90 days). But if in any specific case the government does choose to enforce the letter of the law, there is no right of appeal to the courts, since the person affected has no legal claim to the concession.

Sometimes the state uses powers of 'compulsory purchase' of property from owners, perhaps to clear the land for a new railway line or motorway. This may be fair enough, but governments should never confiscate people's property without proper compensation – for example, because of unproved *suspicion* of involvement in a crime. 'Money-laundering' regulations prevent anonymous transmission of money and force bankers to become state spies. By enabling governments to find out details of anyone's bank accounts, they intrude on *private* property rights.

Restrictions on the market

Further ways in which politics can restrict or obstruct the market include 'nationalised' industries, with which it is illegal for anyone to compete. In recent years, following extensive 'privatisation' of utilities and other state enterprises, widespread regulation has become a major threat to the market system. It need not always stem directly from central government. To give just one example, in 1990 there were about 300 pages of accounting rules, but by 2005 there were about 3,000 pages. A tenfold increase in a mere fifteen years is surely too much. And where will such over-regulation end?

In any country, 'governments', whether 'local', national or supranational, need to provide certain public goods collectively, such as defence and justice. Within reason most people are content to pay for these by means of compulsory demands (taxes). But modern governments levy taxes for other purposes too: to spend on goods that are not really 'public' (in that they could be charged for), such as schooling and health; and to make 'transfer payments', mostly for 'welfare benefits'. Taxation transfers spending power not just from private to public sector, but from individual to collective, from voluntary to coercive. You pays your money and the government imposes its choice.

Some people may be supposed to lack the insight and moral strength to provide for their own future. But then, as Mises says, it is paradoxical to entrust the nation's welfare to the decisions of voters unable to manage their own affairs. Aggregate national statistics can be misleading if there are big regional differences. In some parts of the United Kingdom there may be almost as many 'tax-receivers' as net taxpayers, which implies obvious dangers for a democracy.

If the tax burden gets too high it suppresses incentives. Not so long ago the top rate of tax on quite modest incomes exceeded 90 (ninety!) per cent, which severely hampered the market system. There is no point in 'playing shop', as in a children's game, if the counters you win during the game are taken away at bedtime. But as long as you are free to emigrate from an unpleasant regime – *and take your personal property with you* – you can 'escape'. (That was not possible in the UK.) Thus 'harmonising' rules across different countries can be very damaging. Preventing escape from anti-market laws is like preventing a customer from switching from one supplier to another.

The welfare state: the gentlemen in Whitehall know best

Mises points out that state-worshippers ascribe to government all those qualities which believers ascribe to God – omnipotence, omniscience, infinite goodness. Theirs is a quasi-religious faith and they denounce opponents as wicked. The very term the 'welfare state' aims to imply that those who oppose government control in this important area oppose welfare itself. This is quite untrue: indeed, there is evidence that people would spend *more* on welfare services if they themselves got the benefit directly.

Douglas Jay famously said:

> Housewives as a whole cannot be trusted to buy all the right things, where nutrition and health are concerned. This is really no more than an extension of the principle according to which the housewife herself would not trust a child of four to select the week's purchases. For in the case of nutrition and health, as in the case of education, the gentleman in Whitehall really does know better what is good for people than the people know themselves. (Jay, 1948: 248)

The gentlemen in Whitehall do *not* know best, but even if they did, free adults – not children of four! – might still want to choose for themselves. Freedom means freedom even to make mistakes. Jay's claim seems far fetched, given the different conditions and wishes of millions of people. But even if it were true, that by no means implies that we should all simply obey *orders* from White-hall. It would suffice for the government to *publish* its 'superior' knowledge. Then we could all choose for ourselves whether or not to accept the advice. As Hayek said, market signals are like sign-posts: they tell us where a road leads, without *commanding* us to take it.

The case for reform

The first stage in reforming the welfare state would be for the government to *charge* for services that are currently 'free'. But, depending on their family set-up, everyone would get free vouchers for specific money amounts, earmarked for 'schooling' or 'health'. People would use the vouchers to pay for schooling and health services either from the welfare state or from other providers. They would become customers in a market and could shop around instead of counting for little in the state system. This would give competing producers an incentive to serve customers well.

Even if governments *pay* for social services, they need not *provide* the services. Apart from poor quality, there are political dangers in a state monopoly of schooling. Parents who want their children to attend a non-state school currently have to pay the full cost *twice*: for state schooling via taxes *and* for 'independent' schooling from after-tax income. That is socially divisive: the extra cost severely restricts choice for all but the very rich. Under the voucher system people would only have to pay for the excess cost of independent schooling over the amount of the vouchers.

In time private suppliers would provide more social services and the government less. Schools and hospitals could be profit-seeking; or they could be run by charities, as many were before governments took them over long ago. The government could gradually reduce the money amounts of the vouchers and reduce taxes in line. Since government spending on social services currently accounts for *two-thirds* of all tax revenues, the scope for tax reductions is clearly enormous. Social services are certainly important. So are food and clothing; but that is no reason to make the food and clothing industries state monopolies.

Rather than provide free to all services that most people could afford to pay for if taxes were much lower, it would be better to subsidise poor families directly. This provides more freedom of choice both for poor families and for others, and it also lets suppliers compete and respond to customers' wishes. It is perhaps even more important for poor families than for others to be free to choose how to spend their limited resources. Of course they will not spend their money as the gentlemen in Whitehall think best: no human being could.

When two parties agree to a market exchange, both of them normally expect to benefit. Otherwise they would not choose to undertake the transaction. (As Menger points out, they would probably be unwilling to reverse it.) In other words, as a rule, a market exchange is not a 'zero-sum game' – both parties can gain, and usually do. Hence blocking voluntary trades makes them worse off than they would otherwise be. This applies to imports, drugs or tickets from touts – all things that governments may regard as 'undesirable', even though everyone directly concerned in fact desires them.

There may need to be special rules to protect young children, or others who cannot look after themselves. But some state schools are so bad that many of their pupils are still illiterate when they come on to the jobs market. It would be better to let people leave school when they wanted – as long as they could pass sensible examinations in the three Rs and a few other subjects. Sitting all day in a boring classroom, they not only learn nothing themselves but disrupt lessons for others who do want to study.

The costs of regulation

Freedom for people to spend their money how they like means just that. Governments may decide to prevent freedom of choice by 'criminalising' the purchase or possession of certain drinks or drugs or pornography. But such 'prohibitions' tend to cause more social damage than they prevent. It is the same with restricting the freedom of producers: for example, requiring people to acquire a 'licence' to practise as a doctor or outlawing 'alternative' medicines.

A new drug may promise enormous benefits, but with a slight chance of serious side effects. Regulators who expect the blame if anything goes wrong may be tempted to delay approval until they know the drug is completely safe. But such risk aversion may deprive thousands of patients of the benefits for years. The indirect effects of regulations can be even more important: for example, the jobs that employers *fail* to create because of the potential costs of 'employee-friendly' rules. Those rules may be 'friendly' to *existing* employees but positively hostile to potential *future* employees, who are much less visible.

A specific danger these days is so-called 'anti-discrimination' laws. These derived from a time when nationalised industries were rife and people felt that they – like governments – should treat everyone the same. For instance, if a state auditing monopoly refused to employ someone because she was black, or atheist, she would be unable to practise her profession. In competitive markets, however, if a firm wants to discriminate against hiring people over 50, or Arsenal supporters, it should be free to do so. The 'victim' can always seek a job with many other employers.

One of the most destructive examples of government interference with the freedom of both consumers and producers is imposing price controls. In times of inflation, these limit increases in *money* prices, which in effect requires the seller to *reduce* prices in 'real' terms. If that were a good idea, why not follow the logic of the argument and require the seller to reduce the selling price to *zero*? Price controls not only restrict freedom of exchange on mutually acceptable terms, but they obscure valuable market signals about shortages and surpluses.

The role of the state

The original purpose of governments was to prevent harm by providing defence against external enemies and legal remedies against internal violence. But Herbert Spencer explained that this gradually changed into positively 'doing good', for example by providing 'welfare' services and paying for them out of taxes. In fact most governments are not 'do-gooders' at all – they often do more harm than good – but at best 'mean-wellers'.

Dicey noted:

> The beneficial effect of State intervention ... is direct,
> immediate, and ... visible, whilst its evil effects are
> gradual and indirect and lie outside our sight. ... Hence
> [most people] look with undue favour upon government
> intervention. This natural bias can be counteracted only by
> the existence ... of a presumption or prejudice in favour of
> individual liberty, that is of *laissez-faire*. (Dicey, 1914: 257).

This leads to the 'nightwatchman state', or a minimum of government coercion.

Politics and government failure

Politicians face different incentives from business people. Adam Smith wrote: 'It is not from the benevolence of the butcher, the brewer or the baker, that we expect our dinner, but from their regard to their own interest' (Smith, 1776: 14). That is the 'profit motive'. But most national politicians seem to regard *getting re-elected* as easily the most important thing in their lives. Since the next general election is, on average, only about two years in the future, that means their time horizons are very short. And they like to *appear* to be doing something, so they are always busy interfering.

In contrast, in the market system, people often have reason to take a much longer view: either in progressing their career, saving for their own retirement, perhaps on average some twenty years in the future, or leaving property to their descendants. Moreover people can shop around every day, rewarding or penalising sellers who satisfy them or fail to do so. Nor need we all choose the same: the market caters for minorities as well as the masses.

It is hard to hold politicians to account. True, voters in democracies do have the collective option of 'throwing the rascals out'. But that may just mean letting another lot of rascals in. In most systems you get a vote only once every four years or so; which may allow you a single judgement on a whole range of past actions together with principles or 'promises' for the future. But a promise you cannot enforce legally is unlikely to be worth much.

The European Union, which has now taken over many of the functions of national parliaments, is not itself democratic. There is no way we British can 'throw out' the members of the European Commission. They represent an alien tyranny. And the 'social model' they seem to want to impose is even farther from the free market than the British 'mixed economy'. That is now the largest threat to the market system in the UK.

Another problem with politics is that it can pay pressure groups to invest substantial resources in lobbying. They hope to get large returns because most of the benefits accrue to their own members, whereas the community as a whole bears the costs. The more that governments interfere in the market, the more society is liable to this kind of loss. It is striking how many pressure groups have 'emigrated' to Brussels, where the power is now.

Politicians like talking of 'market failure', but are less willing to acknowledge *government* failures. At least there is a remedy for market failure: incompetent (or unlucky) producers who fail to satisfy consumers make losses and in the end go bankrupt. No such fate awaits governments that fail. The more that politics submerge markets, the less robust and productive the system will be.

Individual responsibility is a vital part of the market system. *Caveat emptor*: 'let the buyer take care'. When people are spending their own money, they tend to take care of it, they try to avoid losses, and think before they act. Not so in the political system, which is truly 'irresponsible'. Moreover people can learn from their own mistakes. We do not learn nearly so much (nor do politicians themselves) from the mistakes of government. As Herbert Spencer said: 'The ultimate result of shielding men from the effects of folly, is to fill the world with fools' (Spencer, 1891).

Conclusion

Governments have got much too large: they spend far too much, especially on welfare services that the market could provide more effectively; they therefore tax far too much, often also imposing a large compliance burden; and they interfere far too much, with regulations that have clearly never been subject to any kind of cost–benefit analysis. Finally, British governments of all parties have handed over intrusive powers to the anti-democratic European Union, with its ratchet-like *acquis communautaire* and Napoleonic legal system. These are all serious dangers to free markets.

Seldon argues that we should regard politics as a useful but specialised and minor service, like dentistry or tree-felling. We should be ready to hire and fire the few politicians required exactly like other employees: they should not stay too long and forget their place. We should regard them with scepticism, not with reverence. Parliament should revert to its nineteenth-century practice of meeting for only a few months each year. And ideally I would say it should also revert to its nineteenth-century practice of taking less than 10 per cent of the national income in taxes.

References

Bullock, A. (1962), *Hitler: a Study in Tyranny*, London: Penguin Books.

Dicey, A. V. (1914), *Lectures on the Relation between Law and Public Opinion during the Nineteenth Century*, London: Macmillan.

Jay, D. (1948), *The Socialist Case*, 2nd edn, London: Faber and Faber.

Schumpeter, J. A. (1954), *Capitalism, Socialism and Democracy*, 4th edn, London: Unwin University Books.

Smith, A. (1776), *The Wealth of Nations*, Book I, ch. II.

Spencer, H. (1891), 'State tamperings with money and banks', in *Essays: Scientific, Political and Speculative*, vol. III, London: Williams and Norgate.

QUESTIONS FOR DISCUSSION

1) What are the essential functions of government? Why?
2) Why have nearly all developed societies rejected socialism and preferred some version of capitalism?
3) Why are enforceable property rights so important to capitalism?
4) Why is significant inequality of personal wealth and incomes a necessary feature of market economies?
5) What are the main functions of market prices? Why are price controls damaging?
6) Was Adam Smith right to say that 'the sole end and purpose of production is consumption'? Are the interests of producers different from those of consumers? How can they be reconciled?
7) Why may the implicit interest rates (time preferences) of democratic politicians vary from those of most adult individuals and families? Does it matter? Why?
8) What, according to Seldon, are 'public goods improper'? How could they be 'privatised'?
9) Bertrand Russell, the famous philosopher, wrote: 'The Industrial Revolution caused unspeakable misery both in England and America. I do not think any student of economic history can doubt that the average happiness in England in

the early 19th century was lower than it had been a hundred years earlier.' Is his view defensible? How could one try to compare the average happiness in England in the early 20th and early 21st centuries?

10) John Stuart Mill, the famous philosopher, wrote: 'It is only in the backward countries of the world that increased production is still an important object.' Do you agree? Why or why not?

11) What are the economic problems engendered by 'free' welfare services such as health and education?

12) How did people cope before the welfare state provided 'free' education, health and pensions?

ABOUT THE IEA

The Institute is a research and educational charity (No. CC 235 351), limited by guarantee. Its mission is to improve understanding of the fundamental institutions of a free society by analysing and expounding the role of markets in solving economic and social problems.

The IEA achieves its mission by:

- a high-quality publishing programme
- conferences, seminars, lectures and other events
- outreach to school and college students
- brokering media introductions and appearances

The IEA, which was established in 1955 by the late Sir Antony Fisher, is an educational charity, not a political organisation. It is independent of any political party or group and does not carry on activities intended to affect support for any political party or candidate in any election or referendum, or at any other time. It is financed by sales of publications, conference fees and voluntary donations.

In addition to its main series of publications the IEA also publishes a quarterly journal, *Economic Affairs*.

The IEA is aided in its work by a distinguished international Academic Advisory Council and an eminent panel of Honorary Fellows. Together with other academics, they review prospective IEA publications, their comments being passed on anonymously to authors. All IEA papers are therefore subject to the same rigorous independent refereeing process as used by leading academic journals.

IEA publications enjoy widespread classroom use and course adoptions in schools and universities. They are also sold throughout the world and often translated/reprinted.

Since 1974 the IEA has helped to create a world-wide network of 100 similar institutions in over 70 countries. They are all independent but share the IEA's mission.

Views expressed in the IEA's publications are those of the authors, not those of the Institute (which has no corporate view), its Managing Trustees, Academic Advisory Council members or senior staff.

Members of the Institute's Academic Advisory Council, Honorary Fellows, Trustees and Staff are listed on the following page.

The Institute gratefully acknowledges financial support for its publications programme and other work from a generous benefaction by the late Alec and Beryl Warren.

85

Other papers recently published by the IEA include:

WHO, What and Why?
Transnational Government, Legitimacy and the World Health Organization
Roger Scruton
Occasional Paper 113; ISBN 0 255 36487 3; £8.00

The World Turned Rightside Up
A New Trading Agenda for the Age of Globalisation
John C. Hulsman
Occasional Paper 114; ISBN 0 255 36495 4; £8.00

The Representation of Business in English Literature
Introduced and edited by Arthur Pollard
Readings 53; ISBN 0 255 36491 1; £12.00

Anti-Liberalism 2000
The Rise of New Millennium Collectivism
David Henderson
Occasional Paper 115; ISBN 0 255 36497 0; £7.50

Capitalism, Morality and Markets
Brian Griffiths, Robert A. Sirico, Norman Barry & Frank Field
Readings 54; ISBN 0 255 36496 2; £7.50

A Conversation with Harris and Seldon
Ralph Harris & Arthur Seldon
Occasional Paper 116; ISBN 0 255 36498 9; £7.50

Malaria and the DDT Story
Richard Tren & Roger Bate
Occasional Paper 117; ISBN 0 255 36499 7; £10.00

A Plea to Economists Who Favour Liberty: Assist the Everyman
Daniel B. Klein
Occasional Paper 118; ISBN 0 255 36501 2; £10.00

The Changing Fortunes of Economic Liberalism

Yesterday, Today and Tomorrow
David Henderson
Occasional Paper 105 (new edition); ISBN 0 255 36520 9; £12.50

The Global Education Industry

Lessons from Private Education in Developing Countries
James Tooley
Hobart Paper 141 (new edition); ISBN 0 255 36503 9; £12.50

Saving Our Streams

*The Role of the Anglers' Conservation Association in
Protecting English and Welsh Rivers*
Roger Bate
Research Monograph 53; ISBN 0 255 36494 6; £10.00

Better Off Out?

The Benefits or Costs of EU Membership
Brian Hindley & Martin Howe
Occasional Paper 99 (new edition); ISBN 0 255 36502 0; £10.00

Buckingham at 25

Freeing the Universities from State Control
Edited by James Tooley
Readings 55; ISBN 0 255 36512 8; £15.00

Lectures on Regulatory and Competition Policy

Irwin M. Stelzer
Occasional Paper 120; ISBN 0 255 36511 X; ,12.50

Misguided Virtue

False Notions of Corporate Social Responsibility
David Henderson
Hobart Paper 142; ISBN 0 255 36510 1; £12.50

HIV and Aids in Schools
The Political Economy of Pressure Groups and Miseducation
Barrie Craven, Pauline Dixon, Gordon Stewart & James Tooley
Occasional Paper 121; ISBN 0 255 36522 5; £10.00

The Road to Serfdom
The Reader's Digest *condensed version*
Friedrich A. Hayek
Occasional Paper 122; ISBN 0 255 36530 6; £7.50

Bastiat's *The Law*
Introduction by Norman Barry
Occasional Paper 123; ISBN 0 255 36509 8; £7.50

A Globalist Manifesto for Public Policy
Charles Calomiris
Occasional Paper 124; ISBN 0 255 36525 x; £7.50

Euthanasia for Death Duties
Putting Inheritance Tax Out of Its Misery
Barry Bracewell-Milnes
Research Monograph 54; ISBN 0 255 36513 6; £10.00

Liberating the Land
The Case for Private Land-use Planning
Mark Pennington
Hobart Paper 143; ISBN 0 255 36508 x; £10.00

IEA Yearbook of Government Performance 2002/2003
Edited by Peter Warburton
Yearbook 1; ISBN 0 255 36532 2; £15.00

Britain's Relative Economic Performance, 1870–1999
Nicholas Crafts
Research Monograph 55; ISBN 0 255 36524 1; £10.00

Should We Have Faith in Central Banks?
Otmar Issing
Occasional Paper 125; ISBN 0 255 36528 4; £7.50

The Dilemma of Democracy
Arthur Seldon
Hobart Paper 136 (reissue); ISBN 0 255 36536 5; £10.00

Capital Controls: a 'Cure' Worse Than the Problem?
Forrest Capie
Research Monograph 56; ISBN 0 255 36506 3; £10.00

The Poverty of 'Development Economics'
Deepak Lal
Hobart Paper 144 (reissue); ISBN 0 255 36519 5; £15.00

Should Britain Join the Euro?
The Chancellor's Five Tests Examined
Patrick Minford
Occasional Paper 126; ISBN 0 255 36527 6; £7.50

Post-Communist Transition: Some Lessons
Leszek Balcerowicz
Occasional Paper 127; ISBN 0 255 36533 0; £7.50

A Tribute to Peter Bauer
John Blundell et al.
Occasional Paper 128; ISBN 0 255 36531 4; £10.00

Employment Tribunals
Their Growth and the Case for Radical Reform
J. R. Shackleton
Hobart Paper 145; ISBN 0 255 36515 2; £10.00

Fifty Economic Fallacies Exposed
Geoffrey E. Wood
Occasional Paper 129; ISBN 0 255 36518 7; £12.50

A Market in Airport Slots

Keith Boyfield (editor), David Starkie, Tom Bass & Barry Humphreys
Readings 56; ISBN 0 255 36505 5; £10.00

Money, Inflation and the Constitutional Position of the Central Bank

Milton Friedman & Charles A. E. Goodhart
Readings 57; ISBN 0 255 36538 1; £10.00

railway.com

Parallels between the Early British Railways and the ICT Revolution
Robert C. B. Miller
Research Monograph 57; ISBN 0 255 36534 9; £12.50

The Regulation of Financial Markets

Edited by Philip Booth & David Currie
Readings 58; ISBN 0 255 36551 9; £12.50

Climate Alarmism Reconsidered

Robert L. Bradley Jr
Hobart Paper 146; ISBN 0 255 36541 1; £12.50

Government Failure: E. G. West on Education

Edited by James Tooley & James Stanfield
Occasional Paper 130; ISBN 0 255 36552 7; £12.50

Waging the War of Ideas

John Blundell
Second edition
Occasional Paper 131; ISBN 0 255 36547 0; £12.50

Corporate Governance: Accountability in the Marketplace

Elaine Sternberg
Second edition
Hobart Paper 147; ISBN 0 255 36542 x; £12.50

The Land Use Planning System
Evaluating Options for Reform
John Corkindale
Hobart Paper 148; ISBN 0 255 36550 0; £10.00

Economy and Virtue
Essays on the Theme of Markets and Morality
Edited by Dennis O'Keeffe
Readings 59; ISBN 0 255 36504 7; £12.50

Free Markets Under Siege
Cartels, Politics and Social Welfare
Richard A. Epstein
Occasional Paper 132; ISBN 0 255 36553 5; £10.00

Unshackling Accountants
D. R. Myddelton
Hobart Paper 149; ISBN 0 255 36559 4; £12.50

The Euro as Politics
Pedro Schwartz
Research Monograph 58; ISBN 0 255 36535 7; £12.50

Pricing Our Roads
Vision and Reality
Stephen Glaister & Daniel J. Graham
Research Monograph 59; ISBN 0 255 36562 4; £10.00

The Role of Business in the Modern World
Progress, Pressures, and Prospects for the Market Economy
David Henderson
Hobart Paper 150; ISBN 0 255 36548 9; £12.50

Public Service Broadcasting Without the BBC?
Alan Peacock
Occasional Paper 133; ISBN 0 255 36565 9; £10.00

The ECB and the Euro: the First Five Years
Otmar Issing
Occasional Paper 134; ISBN 0 255 36555 1; £10.00

Towards a Liberal Utopia?
Edited by Philip Booth
Hobart Paperback 32; ISBN 0 255 36563 2; £15.00

The Way Out of the Pensions Quagmire
Philip Booth & Deborah Cooper
Research Monograph 60; ISBN 0 255 36517 9; £12.50

Black Wednesday
A Re-examination of Britain's Experience in the Exchange Rate Mechanism
Alan Budd
Occasional Paper 135; ISBN 0 255 36566 7; £7.50

Crime: Economic Incentives and Social Networks
Paul Ormerod
Hobart Paper 151; ISBN 0 255 36554 3; £10.00

The Road to Serfdom *with* **The Intellectuals and Socialism**
Friedrich A. Hayek
Occasional Paper 136; ISBN 0 255 36576 4; £10.00

Money and Asset Prices in Boom and Bust
Tim Congdon
Hobart Paper 152; ISBN 0 255 36570 5; £10.00

The Dangers of Bus Re-regulation
and Other Perspectives on Markets in Transport
John Hibbs et al.
Occasional Paper 137; ISBN 0 255 36572 1; £10.00

The New Rural Economy
Change, Dynamism and Government Policy
Berkeley Hill et al.
Occasional Paper 138; ISBN 0 255 36546 2; £15.00

The Benefits of Tax Competition
Richard Teather
Hobart Paper 153; ISBN 0 255 36569 1; £12.50

Wheels of Fortune
Self-funding Infrastructure and the Free Market Case for a Land Tax
Fred Harrison
Hobart Paper 154; ISBN 0 255 36589 6; £12.50

Were 364 Economists All Wrong?
Edited by Philip Booth
Readings 60
ISBN-10: 0 255 36588 8; ISBN-13: 978 0 255 36588 8; £10.00

Europe After the 'No' Votes
Mapping a New Economic Path
Patrick A. Messerlin
Occasional Paper 139
ISBN-10: 0 255 36580 2; ISBN-13: 978 0 255 36580 2; £10.00

The Railways, the Market and the Government
John Hibbs et al.
Readings 61
ISBN-10: 0 255 36567 5; ISBN-13: 978 0 255 36567 3; £12.50

Corruption: The World's Big C
Cases, Causes, Consequences, Cures
Ian Senior
Research Monograph 61
ISBN-10: 0 255 36571 3; ISBN-13: 978 0 255 36571 0; £12.50

Sir Humphrey's Legacy
Facing Up to the Cost of Public Sector Pensions
Neil Record
Hobart Paper 156
ISBN-10: 0 255 36578 0; ISBN-13: 978 0 255 36578 9; £10.00

The Economics of Law
Cento Veljanovski
Second edition
Hobart Paper 157
ISBN-10: 0 255 36561 6; ISBN-13: 978 0 255 36561 1; £12.50

Living with Leviathan
Public Spending, Taxes and Economic Performance
David B. Smith
Hobart Paper 158
ISBN-10: 0 255 36579 9; ISBN-13: 978 0 255 36579 6; £12.50

The Vote Motive
Gordon Tullock
New edition
Hobart Paperback 33
ISBN-10: 0 255 36577 2; ISBN-13: 978 0 255 36577 2; £10.00

Waging the War of Ideas
John Blundell
Third edition
Occasional Paper 131
ISBN-10: 0 255 36606 X; ISBN-13: 978 0 255 36606 9; £12.50

The War Between the State and the Family
How Government Divides and Impoverishes
Patricia Morgan
Hobart Paper 159
ISBN-10: 0 255 36596 9; ISBN-13: 978 0 255 36596 3; £10.00